STURMOVIK

Though the Ilyushin Il-2 needs no introduction, a few words about this remarkable machine have to be said. Nicknamed 'Hunchback' by the Soviets and 'Zementbomber' by the Germans, it was the most produced military aircraft in history - together with its successor, the Il-10, more than 42,000 were built.

The Il-2 was a stable and reliable plane that quickly became a capable anti-tank weapon. The most notable feature was its armoured protection, in particular, armour plates replaced the frame and panelling throughout the nacelle and middle of the fuselage and an armoured hull protected the engine, cockpit, radiators and fuel tanks. Because of this protection, the Il-2 could sustain a great deal of battle damage and proved a challenge for enemy Flak to shoot down. Thanks to the inclusion of a rear-gunner (in the two-seat versions), it could defend itself against attacking fighters, particularly when the 'Sturmoviks' were flying in a defensive formation.

The last variant, the Il-2M3, had maximum speed of 414km/h and effective range of 720km. Its armament included two 23mm wing cannons with 150 rounds per gun, two 7·62mm wing machineguns with 750 rounds per gun, a 12·7mm machinegun in the rear cockpit with 300 rounds, up to 600kg of bombs and eight rockets.

Top: A Sturmovik of the 715th Assault Air Regiment (136th Assault Air Division of the 17th Air Army) taking off from an airfield southwest of Budapest during the battles of 1944/45. This unit was heavily involved in close-support operations on the southern flank of the Eastern Front and its pilots earned a reputation for being tank-busting experts. **RGAKFD**

37mm NS-37

CANNONS

Most Sturmoviks were equipped with 23mm VYa-23 auto-cannons with a rate of fire of about 600 rounds per minute, the highest rate of fire for the calibre at the time. The ammunition included fragmentation-incendiary (OZ), fragmentation-incendiary-tracer (OZT) and armour piercing-incendiary (BZ) rounds.

The BZ round could penetrate 25mm armour at about 400 metres - barely effective against most German AFVs. It could successfully engage armoured cars and halftracks, but did little to medium and heavy Panzers.

A number of Sturmoviks were built as tank busters and fitted with the more powerful 37mm NS-37 auto-cannons in under-wing pods with 50 rounds per gun. At 260 rounds per minute, these had lower rate of fire and could be loaded with high-explosive-fragmentation-incendiary (OFZ) or armour piercing-tracer (BT) rounds.

The BT round could penetrate 40mm armour up to an angle of 45°, but the relatively low rate of fire of the NS-37 gun and the heavy recoil made hitting targets difficult. Pilots were trained to fire short bursts, but on lighter aircraft and because of that only the first shot was actually aimed. Additionally, the penetration of the top armour of the medium and heavy Panzers was possible only at angles above 40°, which was hard to achieve in battle conditions. Accordingly, these NS-37-equipped Sturmoviks were usually flown by experienced pilots with sharp-shooter skills. (Russians called them 'snipers'). When flown by a 'sniper', the tank-busting Il-2 proved a very effective weapon. Attacks were carried out against the rear and upper surfaces of Panzers, where the armour was thinner and penetration easier. Unsurprisingly, shots aimed at these vulnerable areas were successful even against the well-protected Tigers and Panthers.

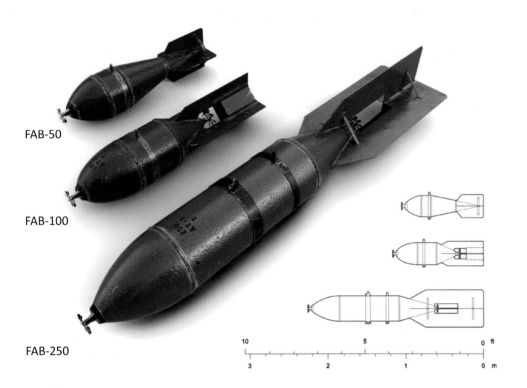

FAB-50

FAB-100

FAB-250

| 10 | | 5 | | 0 ft |
| 3 | 2 | | 1 | 0 m |

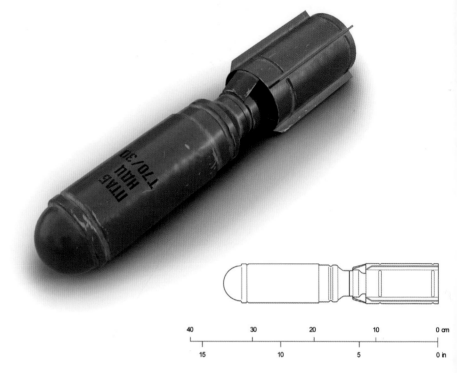

| 40 | 30 | 20 | 10 | 0 cm |
| 15 | | 10 | | 5 | 0 in |

FAB-50/100/250

The Sturmovik could carry up to 600kg of bombs in internal bomb bays and external racks. The most commonly used types against AFVs were FAB (general-purpose), and anti-tank (PTAB).

The FAB-50, FAB-100 and FAB-250 were general-purpose bombs weighing 50, 100 and 250kg, respectively. They had forged-steel body and a tail unit. FAB's were also made from obsolete or captured artillery shells, and received the suffix 'M' (M2 to M9).

Even though the FAB bombs were intended for attack against general targets, they were used with great success against AFVs. A direct hit was not required to put a tank or self-propelled gun out of action - the shrapnel could punch holes in the side armour or damage the running gear. It was rather the structure of the bomb than its weight that proved to be the most decisive factor for tank-busting, as the FAB-50M2, M5 and M9, which were remodelled 149-155mm artillery shells, turned out to be 25% more effective against medium and heavy Panzers than the FAB-100. The reason was simple: the forged-steel body of the original FAB-100 splintered into much lighter and smaller fragments than the shell-based FAB-50M.

PTAB

The shaped-charge PTAB bomb was introduced in the summer of 1943 in order to counter the increasing power of the Panzerwaffe. The weight of the bomb was 2·5kg with 1·5kg of explosives, and because of this was officially designated 'PTAB-2.5-1.5'.

The PTAB could penetrate 60 to 80mm of armour, which was enough to destroy any enemy tank at the time because it generally fell straight on their tops, where armoured protection was least.

Each Sturmovik could carry up to 192 PTABs in four cartridges or up to 220 in four bomb racks. When all PTABs were released at an altitude of 70 to 100 metres, practically every tank in a 15x70 square metre area was hit.

The Soviet High Command was pleasantly surprised by the performance of the PTABs. For instance, it appeared that a group of 15 Il-2's loaded with PTABs could engage a 500 metre long column of armour and motor vehicles, destroying up to 60% of them. In comparison, if the same column was attacked with FAB-50, the same result could only be achieved by 80 Pe-2 dive bombers, i.e. four regiments.

columns and troop concentrations, especially when caught in the open. Conversely, the performance of the RS against AFVs was poor, and the RS-82 could only put a light tank or halftrack out of action with a direct hit. Near misses of a metre or more did not damage armoured vehicles. The RS-132 could destroy medium AFVs with a direct hit, but caused almost no damage to light or medium armoured machines with a near-miss. The situation began to improve from mid-1943, when ROFS-132 and RBS-132 were introduced.

TACTICS

The main tactical formation of the Soviet close-support air force was the assault air division. It was made of three regiments each with 36 Il-2's, although in reality the number was often lower. The regiments operated in 2-12 plane groups that were escorted by 2-4 fighters. (The typical ratio was 3:1.) When in small groups (e.g; four Sturmoviks) they flew unescorted because there were never enough fighters.

The attacking group was led by the most experienced officer. An issue that always was taken into consideration when planning the mission was the enemy anti-aircraft defence. If there was information that the target area was heavily protected by Flak, part of the group was tasked with its destruction. If this information was not available beforehand, and Flak fire was encountered during the attack, the group commander usually detached part of his Sturmoviks to deal with it.

Flying in a tight formation was of paramount importance because it allowed the rear gunners to defend against enemy fighters with well-coordinated 'group fire'. A passive defence measure was used with success against fighters - the Il-2's tried to fly as low as possible, because it was a well-known fact that they where much more vulnerable when being attacked from below, than from above.

The Il-2 groups used three basic types of approach during their attacks. In open terrain and when striking vehicles, artillery positions or advancing enemy infantry, the Sturmoviks would make their attacks at low altitudes, releasing their missiles and firing with their on-board weapons in a near horizontal trajectory. More solid targets, such as buildings and bunkers, would be strafed and bombed using the 'classic' dive-bombing pass (a steep 30 to 40° dive). The third and probably most popular technique was the so-called 'circle of death', in which the Sturmoviks flanked around the enemy, successively dived to make individual attack runs, climbed out to rejoin the formation and dived again. In so doing, the Il-2 was able to protect the tail of the one in the front and at the same time repeatedly attack the target until its ammunition was finished.

Cooperation with ground forces was maintained through a system of forward air controllers and liaison officers with long-range radios and field telephone network.

RS-82

ROFS-132

5

0 ft

2

1

0 m

ROCKETS

The Sturmovik could also carry RS-82 and RS-132 unguided rockets, the numerical suffix referring to their diameter, 82mm and 132mm, respectively. The forward sections contained the warheads and contained 0.36kg (RS-82) and 0.9kg (RS-132) of explosive filler.

The RS rockets were already part of the Soviet arsenal when war broke out. Several variants were subsequently introduced: ROS (fragmentation), ROFS (high-explosive fragmentation), RBS (armour-piercing), ZS (incendiary) and others. These had improved aerodynamics and some had more powerful warheads. The shaped-charge RBS rockets, in particular, were capable of penetrating armour up to 50mm (RS-82) and 75mm (RS-132), respectively.

Although some Il-2's were field-modified to carry up to 24 rockets, the standard load was eight RS-82 or four RS-132. (The latter was heavier at 23kg while the weight of the RS-82 was just 6kg). Like most unguided missiles, the RS suffered from poor accuracy, and in combat situations were typically fired in salvos several hundred metres from the target, thereby increasing the probability of a hit.

The RS were used with success against large ground targets such as soft-skinned transport

North of Simontornya the Germans had set up a solid stronghold comprising up to 40 tanks, 8 motor vehicles and up to 10 field artillery pieces. It was protected by strong Flak fire from Simontornya, Igar and Sáregres. On 18 March 1945 the commander of the 17th Air Army ordered a group of 14 Il-2 of the 639th Assault Air Regiment (189th Assault Air Division) dispatched to that area. It was led by Senior-Lieutenant Tereschenko and was divided into three sub-groups. The group approached the target area at an altitude of 900 metres. The first sub-group formed a 'circle of death' and began to silence the Flak with bombs and on-board weapons. The other two sub-groups also formed their 'circles of death' and attacked targets of their own choice. They made 6 passes and reportedly inflicted heavy loses on the German force.

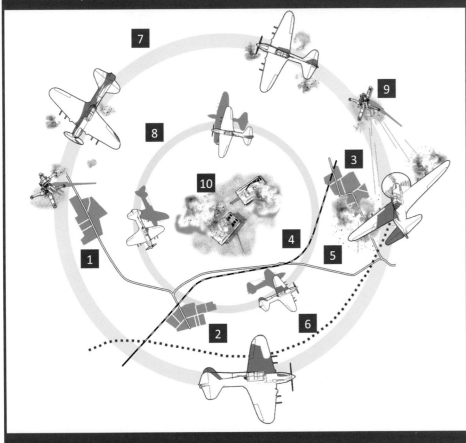

1. Igar
2. Simontornya
3. Sáregres
4. Railway
5. Road
6. Front line
7. 'Circle of death'
8. 'Circle of death'
9. German Flak defences
10. German stronghold

In 1945 the Hungarian lowlands saw the last large-scale tank battles on the Eastern Front. Eventually, the Germans were defeated and left behind large quantities of destroyed Panzers, self-propelled guns, armoured cars and halftracks. The wrecked AFVs provoked a great interest among the Soviets and representatives of all main branches of the 3rd Ukrainian Front toured the battlefields and carried out detailed examinations of many of these vehicles. They rightfully believed that these studies would provide them with plenty of food for thought and would help them in improving their tactical methods.

The first two commissions were formed by the 17th Air Army and the HQ of the artillery of the 3rd Ukrainian Front. They toured the area to the northwest, west and southwest of Budapest from 5 February to 10 March 1945. (It must be kept in mind that by then Germans had managed to recapture some ground, therefore the Soviets were not able to examine a significant number of AFVs they had put out of action during the 1944/45 winter battles.)

From 5 to 23 February 1945 the commission formed by the HQ of the artillery of the 3rd Ukrainian Front visited Buda, as well as most of the recent battlefields as far as Dorog in the northwest, Lake Velence in the southwest and Dunapentele in the south. Its members examined 131 fully tracked German and Hungarian AFVs that had been destroyed between December 1944 and February 1945 by artillery and tank fire. Furthermore, 40 more AFVs (trophy No's 132-172) discovered south of the Lake Velence and in Budafok were also examined immediately after the completion of the report.

The commission formed by the 17th Air Army toured the vast area from Dunaföldvár in the south to Piliscsaba in the north. From 3 to 10 March 1945 its members studied and registered 59 vehicles destroyed in combat since the end of December 1944:

- 28 - by the air force (4 Pz.Kpfw.IV, 8 Panthers, 3 Tiger IIs, 3 self-propelled guns, 4 SPW, 6 motor vehicles)
- 24 - by the artillery (5 Pz.Kpfw.IV, 6 Panthers, 5 Tiger I, 1 Tiger II, 1 Flammpanzer III, 6 self-propelled guns)
- 3 - by tanks (3 Panthers)
- 4 - by anti-tank mines (1 Pz.Kpfw.IV, 3 Panthers)

It is worth mentioning that the photos show that only three tanks (Panther, Tiger I and Tiger II) were claimed by both the artillery and the air force and because of that appear in both studies. All other vehicles listed are unique.

The commission also revealed that in the military storehouses and workshops in Buda, Pest, Sárbogárd, Baracska and the Tárnok railway station there was a considerable number of damaged tanks, self-propelled guns and other Axis heavy weapons that had been towed there either by the Germans or by the Soviet trophy brigades, and were in such a state that it was impossible to determine what kind of weapons had put them out of action.

According to the same report, Sturmovik bombing had destroyed the following vehicles:

- 6 - by PTAB bombs (1 Pz.Kpfw.IV, 3 Panthers, 1 Tiger II, 1 Wespe)
- 1 - by FAB-100 (1 Pz.Kpfw.IV)
- 1 - by FAB-50 and FAB-100 (1 Tiger II)

- 12 - by FAB-50 and PTAB bombs (a column of 6 motor vehicles, 4 SPW, 1 Panther and 1 self-propelled gun)
- 4 - by FAB-100 and PTAB bombs (2 Panthers, 1 Tiger II, 1 Hummel)

Up to ten more Panthers and assault guns had been destroyed by PTABs or undisclosed missiles.

The 17th Air Army commission came to the following conclusions:

1. PTAB bombs are the most effective air-to-ground anti-tank weapon.
2. The most vulnerable part of German tanks is the engine compartment. Even a single hit there by a 45mm round is enough to put the tank out of action.
3. The on-board cannons of the Sturmoviks (VYa and ShVAK) can put a tank out of action only if it is attacked into the engine compartment from above.
4. When PTAB bombs score a hit on a tank they always succeed in putting the later out of action.
5. The FAB-50/100 are effective against tanks either when they score a direct hit or when they explode no more than 2 m from them. In all other cases they are ineffective.

Another commission was formed by the 17th Air Army immediately after the end of the spring battles between the Lakes Balaton and Velence. From 24 March to 20 April 1945 it toured the battlefields and inspected 430 fully tracked Axis AFVs that had been destroyed between December 1944 and March 1945:

- 7 Pz.Kpfw.IIIs
- 56 Pz.Kpfw.IVs
- 110 Panthers
- 2 Tiger Is
- 39 Tiger IIs
- 27 Jagdpanzer 38s
- 23 self-propelled howitzers on Pz II and Pz.Kpfw.IV chassis
- 12 Jagdpanthers
- 25 assault guns on Pz.Kpfw.III chassis
- 63 assault guns/tank destroyers on Pz.Kpfw.IV chassis
- 12 Pz IIb (presumably Marder-type self-propelled guns)
- 12 Flakpanzers
- 17 Bergepanthers
- 24 Hungarian light tanks

The commission also visited the Vienna Arsenal, where it inspected 148 wrecked AFVs that had been evacuated from the battlefield, but it was impossible to determine what kind of weapons had knocked them out, because many had been cannibalised for spare parts.

The 430 AFVs were destroyed by the following means:

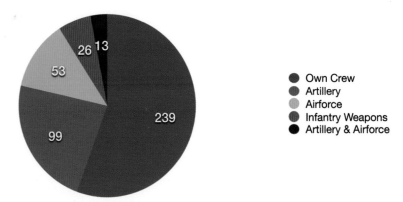

Not surprisingly, it was the 66 (53 + 13) AFVs claimed by the airforce that interested the commission most. An examination of these wrecks gave them plenty of information about the effectiveness of the weapons used by the Sturmoviks. Interestingly, it appeared that the greatest share belonged not to PTABs, which had caused the destruction of 23 vehicles, but to FAB bombs, which accounted for 26. It also turned out that cannons (23mm and 37mm) and ROFS-132 rockets had achieved similar scores - 9 and 8, respectively.

The breakdown by AFV type was as follows:

26 by FAB-250/100/50 (2 Pz.Kpfw.IV, 9 Panthers, 1 assault gun on Pz.Kpfw.III chassis, 8 assault guns on Pz.Kpfw.IV chassis, 3 howitzers on Pz II/IV chassis, 3 Jagdpanzer 38s)
23 by PTAB (1 Pz.Kpfw.III, 3 Pz.Kpfw.IV, 5 Panthers, 3 Tiger IIs, 6 assault guns on Pz.Kpfw.III chassis, 2 assault guns on Pz.Kpfw.IV chassis, 1 howitzer on Pz II/IV chassis, 2 Jagdpanzer 38s)
9 by 23/37mm rounds (2 Panthers, 4 assault guns on Pz.Kpfw.IV chassis, 1 howitzer on Pz II/IV chassis, 2 Jagdpanzer 38s)
8 by ROFS-132 (1 Panther, 1 assault gun on Pz.Kpfw.III chassis, 3 assault guns on Pz.Kpfw.IV chassis, howitzers on Pz II/IV chassis, 1 Jagdpanzer 38)

The two commissions mentioned above were not the only ones that toured the battlefields of Western Hungary in the spring of 1945. The 9th Guards Army, for instance, formed a commission to examine the Panzers destroyed by its units in the area west of Zámoly and assigned its own trophy numbers to them (starting with '1'). The 18th Tank Corps also inspected the wrecks of 35 German AFVs put out of action by its tanks on 24 March 1945 at Tótvázsony. On 23 March 1945 the 6th Guards Tank Army captured 70 severely damaged AFVs loaded on railcars at Veszprém railway station, which, apparently were not studied in any detail.

Thanks to Kamen Nevenkin for this insight into the weapons and tactics used to destroy the Panzers in this book.

A le.Pz.Sp.Wg. Sd.Kfz.222 Ausf.B of St./SS-Pz.Aufkl.Abt.3 knocked out by two hits from a Sturmovik's 23mm cannon at the northern edge of Sárkeresztes between 16 and 18 March 1945. It looks as if scavengers have been picking at the wreck as it is without wheels, muzzle brake and all the engine bay's hatches are open - clearly they had no use for the bucket though. The two piece armoured body identifies this as a 5.Serie vehicle, the last of its type.

3 The northern outskirts of Ozora, at the crossing on the northern bank of Sio canal, a Pz.Kpfw.IV Ausf.J from SS-Pz.Rgt.12, 12.SS-Panzer-Division, tactical number '539', has been destroyed by a FAB-50M9 bomb and an 85mm tank round. The bomb detonated under the right track, damaging it and destroying the first roadwheel while the 85mm round penetrated the armour immediately to the right of the driver's hatch. The Panzer was one of three from 5.Kompanie knocked out by the Soviets while trying to break into Ozora on 11 March 1945.

5 A low frontal view of a Panzer IV/70(V) destroyed around 21 March 1945 in the centre of Lepsény. It had a tactical number '22', which suggests that it belonged to 2./Pz.Jg.Abt.70 of 4.Kavallerie-Division. It was destroyed by a FAB-100 bomb which exploded a metre from the vehicle. On the right side of the hull there were several gouges made by 76mm artillery rounds, but they caused no damage. This vehicle was not fitted with an external gun travel lock, or at least it and its mounts on the bow are missing. The 'arc' shaped gunsight shutter sits on top of the glacis plate. **Below:** A close-up of the rear corner of the fighting compartment shows the damage done to the 40mm thick armour plate - a bomb splinter had caused an explosion inside the vehicle. Note how thin the armour was at the bottom of the sponson. This unusually close view shows the split pins used to hold the track pins in place.

6 The Füle - Balatonfőkajár road, near Hill 162. A MIAG built Sturmgeschütz.III Ausf.G with welded gun mantlet, typical of Stugs from 3.Kavallerie-Division, 3. and 23.Panzer-Divisions who were all in the area. It was destroyed on 21 or 22 March 1945 by a direct hit from a FAB-100 bomb to the engine compartment, which has blown the roof to the side of the road where it now lies upside down. There is also a gouge in the front armour made by a ricocheted 76mm artillery round. The Sturmgeschütz has been field-modified with a generous application of concrete on the front of the fighting compartment, complete with inlaid tracks. More tracks, German and Russian, offered a little extra protection on the front and sides. The method of covering the bow armour with two bracketed rows of tracks bears a resemblance to the example on page 49 of Panzerwrecks 7, and it may be from the same unit.

10/11 A Bergepanther (assembled by Demag between September and November 1944) knocked out while recovering a Panther, probably during the hurried German withdrawal on 22-23 March 1945. The location is the eastern slope of Hill 173 (south of Berhida and immediately to the north of Küngös). The Bergepanther most likely belonged to Pz.Rgt.1 of 1.Panzer-Division, whose Berge-Staffel began to tow knocked-out Panzers left in the area towards Veszprém on 21 March. The pair were destroyed by a blast from an FAB-100 bomb, which exploded a metre away, blowing off the Panther's turret (which had previously been put out of action by a 76mm round that penetrated the right side of the hull).

12 On the eastern edge of Balatonfőkajár lies a Panther Ausf.A, whose chassis had been slightly damaged by a FAB-50 bomb probably around 21-22 March 1945, during the German retreat from this area. Despite the minor damage, the tank was abandoned by the crew. The Russian commission found several bomb craters (FAB-50, AO-25 and PTAB) within 10 metres of the tank. We presume that the Panther belonged to Pz.Rgt.23, 23.Panzer-Division, which even at this stage of the war was still using older models. It has been painted with a coat of whitewash, as some remains on the mantlet and gun mount. The spare tracks on the turret side carry a tactical number.

15 A Jagdpanzer 38 east of Balatonszabadi that received a direct hit from a FAB-100 bomb on the back end, smashing the track, idler, last roadwheel and holing the side of the engine compartment. It belonged to the Hungarian 20. Assault Gun Battalion and was lost during the heavy fighting in the area from 10 to 18 March 1945. The vehicle has features typical of the August 1944 production run.

16 Another Jagdpanzer 38, 700 metres east of Balatonszabadi, has received two direct hits in the engine compartment from PTAB bombs, as result of which it has burnt out completely. It belonged to the Hungarian 20. Assault Gun Battalion and like the vehicle opposite was lost between 10 and 18 March 1945. Its tactical number was '005' (presumably 'T-005'). The slogan *'Előre a Kárpátokig!"* (Forward to the Carpathians!) has been painted onto the frontal armour.

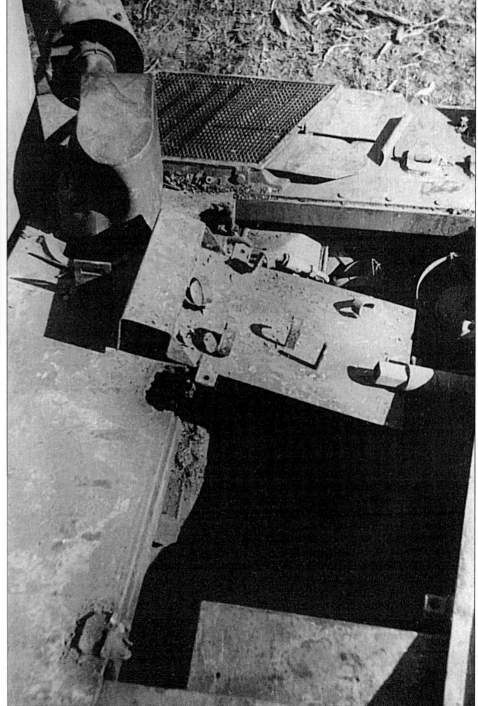

26 This Pz.Kpfw.IV Ausf.J, which presumably belonged to 1.Panzer-Division (23.Panzer-Division was also in the area), was knocked out southeast of Balatonkenese by PTAB bombs, one of which penetrated the corner of the turret and driver's hatch. It was part of a column of at least three Pz.Kpfw. IV's ambushed by Soviet artillery and finished off by Sturmoviks. The chalk writing says: "*Uchteno, Chilikin*" (Counted by Chilikin) and the date. On the ground is the rarely seen frame and mesh base that was added inside the rear of the turret Schürzen to increase stowage. The tank features the tow coupling introduced after December 1944.

31/2 Three PTAB bombs penetrated the engine compartment, chassis and turret, peeling this Pz.Kpfw.IV Ausf.J apart and burning it out. This was a late production vehicle with 'Flammentöter' exhaust mufflers, mounts for 'Drahtgeflecht Schürzen' and final pattern return rollers.

The small rectangular object attached to the turret roof is one of three gas detection panels. Given the location (the southeastern outskirts of Csajág), the Panzer, tactical number '61x' probably belonged to Pz.Rgt.6 of 3.Panzer-Division and was lost on 22 or 23 March 1945. *"Ucht. 31/2"* (Count.[ed] 31/2) has been chalked onto the driver's side armour.

32 On the western edge of Akarattya (Balatonakarattya), a Flakpanzer IV 'Möbelwagen' took on the Sturmoviks and lost, falling victim to 37mm aircraft cannon fire and RS rockets. Soviet artillery weighed in to the fight, with a round penetrating the left wall. The vehicle carried the tactical number '37', probably belonged to s.H.Pz.Abt.509 and was likely destroyed on 23 March 1945. The 3,7cm Flak 43 has been blown from the vehicle and now lays on the ground (to the left of the photo). The radio aerial was fitted on a pivoting mount which angled the aerial backwards as the rear fighting compartment armoured wall was lowered, so that it did not get damaged when traversing and firing the gun. This can be clearly seen here.

32 The same Flakpanzer with the left armour wall raised to the travelling position and displaying the hole made by the Russian artillery round. The thickness of the armour plate was 25mm and the circular hole was a firing port for close defence. Fire has consumed tyres and paintwork alike.

33 Another Flakpanzer IV at Akarattya, also presumed destroyed on 23 March 1945. (It seems that both Flakpanzers had attempted to provide AA cover and were 'silenced' by the Sturmoviks). This one took an ROFS-132 rocket into the right wall of the fighting compartment, shattering it and a hit (circled in white) in the area of the rear return roller. The walls of the fighting compartment had been fixed in the partially opened position and remnants of a whitewash can be seen on the sides along with *"Trofeinaya komanda"* (Trophy command) followed by the name of the trophy unit commander, which is impossible to read.

33 A close up of the side shows the large hole in the right wall. The two square objects to the left of the number '33' are where the stays for the walls should be fitted, instead just these two metal mounts remain. These stays kept the walls in position when flattened to form a deck for the crew and locked into the small brackets just above the trackguard. The Russian technical team has roped open the engine access hatch.

**34** A Jagdpanther at Balatonkenese railway station, destroyed by a direct hit from a FAB-100 bomb, which struck the roof. Another bomb struck the commander's hatch, but made only a dent, and the gun mantlet was penetrated by a 76mm artillery round. It is not clear which unit the tank-destroyer belonged to: s.Pz.Jg.Abt.560, 2.SS-Panzer-Division or 9.SS-Panzer-Division. The area was overrun by Soviet forces on 23 March 1945, but it is probable that the Jagdpanther was knocked out earlier and towed there to be evacuated by rail.

35 This Panther Ausf.G, completed by Daimler-Benz in December 1944, was found at Balatonkenese railway station after being destroyed by PTAB bombs - one of which has penetrated the side armour and burst the interlocking weld seam. The tank, tactical number '212', was the mount of Uscharf Werner Schreber of 2./SS-Pz.Rgt.1, 1.SS-Panzer-Division and issued prior to the Balaton offensive. Like the Jagdpanther opposite, it was probably knocked out earlier and then towed to the station for rail evacuation. The ring on the cupola for the 'Fliegerbeschussgerät' was lost in combat, as earlier photos show this in place.

 Another of 2./SS-Pz.Rgt.1's Daimler-Benz Panthers, this one tactical number '222', abandoned at Balatonkenese railway station after being destroyed 37mm aircraft-cannon fire to the turret, which set off the ammunition. The idler wheel is missing and a chunk of tyre has come away from the rear roadwheel. Note the 'Flammenvernichter' mufflers hanging off the back of the tank. This tank was a replacement for Oscha. Walter Ropeter's Panther lost at Stoumont on 19 December 1944.

36 This close-up shows where the 37mm aircraft cannon penetrated the junction of the turret roof and side, 'cooking off' the ammunition stowed in the sponson next to the driver's position. It is probable that the driver escaped, as his hatch has been jettisoned.

47 On a roadside 2·5km west of Cece, a Panther Ausf.G destroyed by three FAB-100 bombs and two 85mm tank rounds. Two of the bombs exploded 50 metres from the tank, the third hit the engine compartment. We think that it was probably immobilised by Soviet tank fire and then attacked by Sturmoviks, although it could be the other way round. It was lost between 10 and 15 March 1945 and belonged to II./Pz.Rgt.23 of 23.Panzer-Division (the spare tracks and lack of MG ring are identifiers). Like many wrecked Panthers, this one has sunk onto its belly armour due to the torsion bar suspension weakening under extreme heat.

47 The other side of the Panther shows catastrophic destruction. Something has buckled the driver's roof armour inward - possibly one of the 85mm rounds - and an explosion within the ammunition bin has blown out part of the turret side, unseating it in the process. An interesting detail: the turret has parallel cut rear edges to the sides indicating that it was manufactured by Eisenwerke Oberdonnau in Linz.

48 This Jagdpanzer IV was hit by a FAB-50M9 bomb in the engine compartment. The bomb had been dropped from a low altitude and bounced twice before exploding. Adding to the destructive mix were two artillery hits, one penetrating the right-side armour, the other damaging the track. Around the vehicle there were bomb craters of various sizes. The vehicle was found at Hill 120, 3km southeast of Simontornya and presumably lost between 14 and 16 March 1945. It belonged to Pz.Jg.Abt.128 of 23.Panzer-Division, although according to the commission, the tactical number painted on it was strange: '467'. The Jagdpanzer was assembled in September 1944 as it has no 'Zimmerit' coating and would have been one of the last of its type before the switch over to the Panzer IV/70(V) with its long Pak 42 L/70 gun. It was issued to the Abteilung in October 1944 and predominately used in the assault-gun role.

48 Two of the holes made by the FAB-50M9 bomb in the 20mm thick armour plate. The lower one has penetrated the area of the idler mount, although we cannot be sure if the idler was fitted at the time. The tow cable fitted to the rear tow point would indicate that recovery was attempted. The 'Schürzen' on the side of the engine compartment have a couple of unusual additions: a rod welded to the bottom to hold it in place and a pair of tie downs. The exhausts have the appearance of a field modification rather than factory fitted 'Flamentöter' mufflers, as they appear too 'thin'.

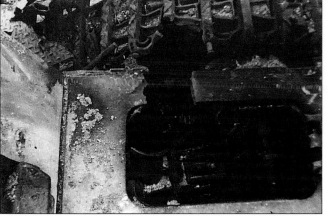

 Between 10 and 15 March 1945, this Pz.Kpfw.IV Ausf.J became stuck in the Soviet trenches immediately to the south of the Simontornya - Cece railway line, 2km east of Simontornya station, and was finished off by several PTAB bomb hits in the engine compartment. Three craters made by more PTABs were found within a radius of 2 metres around the vehicle. Given the location, it belonged either to Pz.Rgt.23, 23.Panzer-Division or SS-Pz.Rgt.1, 1.SS-Panzer-Division. In the background, at the base of the railway embankment, is a knocked out halftrack, shown on page 30. The image on the left shows the damage done to the final drive.

49A This is the halftrack seen in the background of page 28; a Sd.Kfz.250 Ausf.B. The caption with the photo gives the location as the Berhida, not northeast of Simontornya as given in the previous photo. Misidentifications such as this were commonplace across most armies. The rail embankment is visible through the front visors meaning that the left side wall has been blown away by a direct hit from an RS-82 rocket.

50 This Daimler-Benz Panther was a victim of a combined air and artillery attack 2km east of Simontornya. A 76mm artillery round wrecked the idler and immediately next to this was a crater from a FAB-50 bomb. Furthermore, the tank was strafed by VYa 23mm aircraft cannon. Like other wrecks at Simontornya, the kill most probably took place between 10 and 15 March 1945 and belonged to II./Pz.Rgt.23 of 23.Panzer-Division. Note the spare tracks on the turret side and lack of cupola MG rings, both typical features of II./Pz.Rgt.23 Panthers.

51 A Flakpanzer IV 'Möbelwagen', tactical number '925' has nose-dived into a ditch about 100 metres north of Káloz and destroyed by a combination of 76mm artillery and 37mm aircraft cannon fire. It belonged to 1.SS-Panzer-Division and was probably lost on 7-8 March 1945. Apparently the Germans considered it beyond recovery and it has been partially stripped, as the tracks and final drive have gone. It had been given a complete coat of whitewash, including inside the fighting compartment, and the original paint can be seen where the shovel was stowed on the hull side.

55 This Daimler-Benz Panther Ausf.G was knocked out by Sturmoviks to the west of the forest at Felsősárréti-major (northeast of Soponya). It was hit by a FAB-50M9 bomb and the track damaged, fuel tank penetrated and the Panther burned. It is very difficult to say which unit the tank belonged to, but the white camouflage suggests that it was probably lost between 10 and 15 February 1945, during the German counterattacks, in which the main player was 6.Panzer-Division. After this counterattack the battlefield remained in German hands and they probably attempted to recover the tank - a tow clevis is ready for use on the front. The Panther was prepared for infra-red night fighting equipment because the door of the armoured box on the rear wall is visible.

55 A close-up of the damage caused by the FAB-50M9 bomb shows that the hull armour has been penetrated and the idler and track damaged. It is interesting to note that Daimler-Benz did not fit the self cleaning idler to its Panthers.

 A I./Pz.Rgt.24 Panther destroyed on 20-21 March 1945, at the eastern limits of Börgönd by two PTAB bombs and an 85mm tank round. The tank is noteworthy for having the spare tracks fitted to the turret the opposite way round to most - with the track horns facing inwards and a tactical number '121' has been painted onto one of these sections. The engine compartment either has sustained damage, possibly from the PTAB bombs, or has been searched for spare parts afterwards because an air filter lies in the foreground and the rear engine access hatch lies behind the tank. The Panther was assembled by Daimler-Benz in early December 1944.

 Rocket-firing Jabos were not exclusive to the campaign in the west - they killed their fair share of Panzers in the east too. A case in point is this Panzer IV/70(V), knocked out at the Veszprém - Várpalota - Berhida road junction by a direct hit from a ROFS-132 rocket. The resulting explosion has completely blown out the side of the fighting compartment and reduced the roadwheel tyres to ash. The technical team's report states that the rocket hit the engine compartment, but that large hole next to the driver's visor would seem to be the most likely point of entry. The vehicle was probably from SS-Pz.Jg.Abt.1 of 1.SS-Panzer-Division and lost on 22 or 23 March 1945.

 A Panzer IV/70(V), tactical number '311', from SS-Pz.Jg.Abt.1 destroyed by PTAB bombs 800 metres east of Devecser, presumably on 25-26 March 1945. One of its suspension bogies has been damaged and is missing a wheel. An internal explosion has unseated the roof of the fighting compartment and eagle-eyed readers will have spotted that the end of the gun barrel has been destroyed.

85 Panther Ausf.A '524' of SS-Pz.Rgt.5, 5.SS-Panzer-Division, was placed behind an earth berm and used in a static role on the outskirts of Várpalota. The tank was attacked with a number of FAB-100 bombs, one of which scored a direct hit, while two others detonated within 50 metres. What finally destroyed the Panther was a 37mm round from an aircraft cannon, which penetrated the rear turret hatch, setting the ammunition on fire and as a result the tank burnt out. The date of this action was around 22 March 1945. Like many of the Panthers on previous pages, it has liberal amounts of spare track hanging from the turret and more than usual fitted to the rear hull sides. The 'Zimmerit' pattern identifies this as a tank assembled by M.N.H. in the Spring of 1944.

103 This Panzer IV/70(V) was blown apart by a FAB-250 that had landed right on top of the vehicle. It was found at Balatonfűzfő railway station on 23 March 1945, when the area was overrun by the Soviets. Taking into account that the area looks like a scrap yard (note the turretless Panther in the background), it is quite probable that the Panzer had been knocked out earlier and towed here to be evacuated by rail. One of the tracks has been 'short-tracked', making towing much easier.

110 A Jagdpanzer 38 photographed approximately 1km north of Balatonfűzfő, on the road to Veszprém. It was knocked out by the blast from two FAB-250 bombs, pushing the Jagdpanzer into the muddy quagmire that we now see it in. This Škoda-built vehicle belonged to the Hungarian 20. Rohamtüzér Osztály (20. Assault Gun Battalion) and was presumably lost on 23 March 1945 during the fighting withdrawal of Axis troops. Hungarian Jagdpanzers can be identified from German by the large tactical number at the top of the side. Everything else remained the same: camouflage pattern, fittings, even the German 'Balkenkreuz'.

114 Another Jagdpanzer 38, this one destroyed by four PTAB bombs and a 76mm artillery round 2km south of Berhida. The artillery round penetrated the right side of the hull and the bombs went through the roof armour. The Jagdpanzer probably belonged to 44.Reichsgrenadier-Division and was lost on 22-23 March 1945. The photo on this page shows how the PTAB bombs with their shaped-charge warheads had no difficulty in penetrating the Jagdpanzer's armour on the roof and engine deck. This caused the ammunition to explode, blowing off the gunsight cover (which has come to rest on the glacis plate) and driver's periscopes - with these gone we can see how the armour was machined to accommodate the differing angles of the two periscopes. The penetration of the hull side next to the commander's position, helpfully circled in white, was courtesy of the 76mm round. Three of the crew lie dead next to the vehicle.

117

22-23 March 1945. A late production Sturmhaubitze 42 with co-axial MG and no muzzle brake from Heeres Sturmartillerie-Brigade.303 or 3.Kavallerie-Division after a direct hit from an ROFS-132 rocket at Hill 173, 3·5km south of Berhida. The fighting compartment roof has been blown in front of the vehicle and the engine deck upended. It looks as if the rocket hit the StuH in the running gear on the right side and this has either caused the ammunition to explode or disabled the vehicle and the crew set demolition charges. To the right of the photo are the remains of a truck.

119 We can only speculate how this scene would have played out at Hill 173, south of Berhida, after this Panzer IV/70(V) was hit by a FAB-50M9 bomb and three 37mm aircraft-cannon rounds in its engine compartment. The ammunition has 'cooked-off', throwing the roof off and scattering now spent shell casings around. The Panzer has three return rollers but a full set of rubber-tyred roadwheels.

121 2km south of Berhida, a late production Sturmgeschütz III destroyed by a direct hit from a FAB-50M9 bomb in the engine compartment on 22-23 March 1945. The Stug subsequently caught fire and the ammunition detonated. With the tactical number '711', it was part of a tank unit and 7./SS-Pz.Rgt.9 is the most likely candidate, although the insignia on the bow is new to us. The extreme angle of the gun barrel and mantlet could indicate that a demolition charge had been set off in the breech of the gun. It looks like the vehicle has become mired and attempted to reverse out, as the light coloured earth is stuck in the upper track-run.

125 Not far from the vehicle the on page 46 (this one was found 4km south of Berhida), another Sturmgeschütz destroyed by PTAB bombs on the engine compartment. This vehicle does not have the unit insignia or tactical number seen on the previous page and the style of 'Balkenkreuz' is different. In the background, Russian troops inspect a Pz.Kpfw.IV that does not appear in the report.

130 Looking like a range target, a Panther Ausf.G photographed 400 metres south of Pákozd after being destroyed by artillery fire and aerial attack. A 76mm artillery round holed the armour in front of the driver and a bomb had made the large hole and the 37mm cannon the holes in the side of the turret and hull. (It was probably knocked out at short range by the 76mm gun and then finished off by Sturmoviks.) The assault has stripped the front hull side of its tool brackets and broken the track in two places. It is impossible to tell which unit the Panther belonged to or when it was destroyed, because the battles in this area lasted from 20 December 1944 until 20 March 1945.

174 A Daimler-Benz Panther Ausf.G from I./Pz.Rgt.24, destroyed northeast of Székesfehérvár by PTAB bombs and 37mm aircraft-cannon. Tracks had at one point been fitted to the hooks on the turret sides, but a bomb blast - probably the one that made the hole in the turret side - has blown them off along with their hooks. The Panther was most likely lost between 1 and 4 February 1945 when I./Pz.Rgt.24, being tactically subordinated to 3.SS-Panzer-Division, launched a series of counterattacks north and northeast of Szekesfehervar. The earth in front of the tank has been dug out to quite a depth, as the soil is a different colour and could indicate that after the stabilisation of the front along the edge of the town it was incorporated into the Axis defensive system and used as a strongpoint.

50

175 Obliterated by a direct hit from a FAB-100 bomb east of Székesfehérvár was this Panzer IV/70(A) from 8./Pz.Rgt.6, 3.Panzer-Division, destroyed between 21 and 23 December 1944. The vehicle is an early example as it had been given a coat 'Zimmerit', visible on the front of the fighting compartment, and this was omitted after the September production run. The placement of the 'Balkenkreuz' at the top of the glacis is standard for this type of vehicle and the two hooks above would indicate that tracks had been hung over it.

179 On the eastern edge of Seregélyes, the turret and hull of a Panther Ausf.G have been separated by a direct hit from a FAB 100 bomb in the engine compartment. The tank, assembled in July 1944 by M.N.H., probably belonged to I./Pz.Rgt.1, 1.Panzer-Division or I./Pz.Rgt.6, 3.Panzer-Division and was lost between 7 and 20 March 1945. Two more tanks are visible in the background but the quality of the photo does not permit identification.

182 Rare Panzer. A Pz.Beob.Wg.IV destroyed by a FAB-100 bomb at the northern edge of Seregélyes. (The bomb penetrated the engine compartment hatch and detonated inside). Externally these vehicles differed from the regular Pz.Kpfw.IV by having a cupola from a Sturmgeschütz, an extra radio antenna (Sternantenne D) in a 'pot-mount' at the rear of vehicle and one on the turret roof. It was lost between 7 and 20 March 1945 and belonged to Pz.Art.Rgt.73 of 1.Panzer-Division or Pz.Art.Rgt.76 of 6.Panzer-Division.

183 Another rare Panzer, this one a Panther Ausf.G fitted with an armoured box on the rear wall of the hull to take the electrical equipment for infra-red fighting equipment. The turret has been blown apart - the effect of being hit by a FAB-100 bomb in the forward part of the engine compartment. Location: 1km north of Seregélyes. The tank had been painted with a whitewash, some of which remains on the side of the mantlet, wheels and IR box. The winter camouflage and the location suggest that it could have been a vehicle from I./Pz.Rgt.1, 1.Panzer-Division or I./Pz.Rgt.6, 3.Panzer-Division and lost between 3 and 8 February 1945. At this point both units had some IR-ready Panthers (Pz.Rgt.1's had been taken over from I./Pz.Rgt.130). The same units were employed in the same area between 7 and 20 March 1945.

188 Another Panther dismembered by a FAB-100 bomb, this one exploding on the turret roof. The tank, which had the tactical number '405', was found In Szabadbattyán. It is almost impossible to say which unit it belonged to and when it was destroyed because fighting in the area was almost continuous from 22 December 1944 to 22 March 1945.

189

A Pz.Kpfw.IV Ausf.J that may have been in the process of recovery when destroyed. The running gear has been 'short-tracked', by-passing the drive sprocket, which would make the disabled vehicle easier to tow, but the Russian airforce and their PTAB bombs prevented this. One of them hit and penetrated the engine compartment and rendered the tank useless, the resulting fire burning the rubber tyres off the roadwheels. The retreating Germans attempted to demolish the main gun with an explosive charge, note how the muzzle brake is at an angle. Several craters from PTAB bombs were visible around the tank. The white paint scheme was applied by the Russians to prevent accidents in poor visibility.

196 The bare bones of a Tiger II photographed in Polgárdi. From December 1944 to March 1945 this area changed hands three times and during that time the monster was gradually stripped of everything worthwhile. According to the Russian report, the tank was hit by PTAB bombs that penetrated the turret roof and detonated the ammunition. Actually the tank, tactical number '124' of 1./s.H.Pz.Abt.503, was destroyed on 8 December 1944 by a short range hit from a Russian anti-tank gun from 62nd Guards Rifle Division, the round penetrating the driver's position killing him and the radio operator (this has been marked in white by the Russian technical team, although no mention is made of it). As the technical team was looking primarily for evidence of aerial attack, they noted that the roof had been penetrated by PTAB bombs, which must have occurred at a later date. Thanks to Yann Youault for getting to the bottom of this.

240

Tiger '133', from 1./s.H.Pz.Abt.503, was lost on 23 December 1944 during the German counterattack to recapture Úrhida (a village halfway between Nádasdladány and Szabadbattyán). What exactly 'killed' it is a mystery: German sources say it was hit by a hidden 76mm anti-tank gun. On the other hand, the 17th Air Army commission who inspected it in the spring of 1945, reported that it had been hit by three PTAB bombs in the engine compartment and burned out. Furthermore, within 50 metres were two FAB-100 bomb craters. The wreck itself was located about 700 metres east of Úrhida. The wreck was clearly a donor for spare parts as the area was recaptured by the Germans in January 1945.

246 North of Nádasdladány, a Panther Ausf.G from SS-Pz.Rgt.9 has lost the back end of its running gear after being hit by a FAB-100 bomb that severely damaged the left track. There is also a significant damage to the right side: broken track, missing wheels, blown out sponson, etc. Regarding the six penetrations to the turret and hull side, the report says that they were made when a new type of armour-piercing discarding sabot (APDS) round being tested by the Soviets. The Panther was lost during the heavy fighting on 22 March 1945 and is possibly a veteran of the Ardennes Offensive or even Market Garden.

249 A Jagdpanzer 38 probably from 44.Reichsgrenadier-Division that was destroyed on 22 March 1945 by a FAB-100 hitting the engine compartment - note the white circled area on the side. Something, possibly shrapnel, has broken the track, the teeth on the bottom of the drive sprocket and the first roadwheel - which has been marked in white by the Russians.

249 The hole in the side of the engine compartment shows where exactly the 100kg aerial bomb scored a direct hit. Behind this armour plate was the air inlet for the engine and the vehicle radio mounted in the firewall. The vehicle burnt out, probably from the fuel tank catching fire as there is charring on the loader's hatch. The three 'studs' visible above the penetration covered holes in the side for fitting an extra antenna for a FuG 8 radio set that permitted a Jagdpanzer 38 to be converted to a Befehlspanzer.

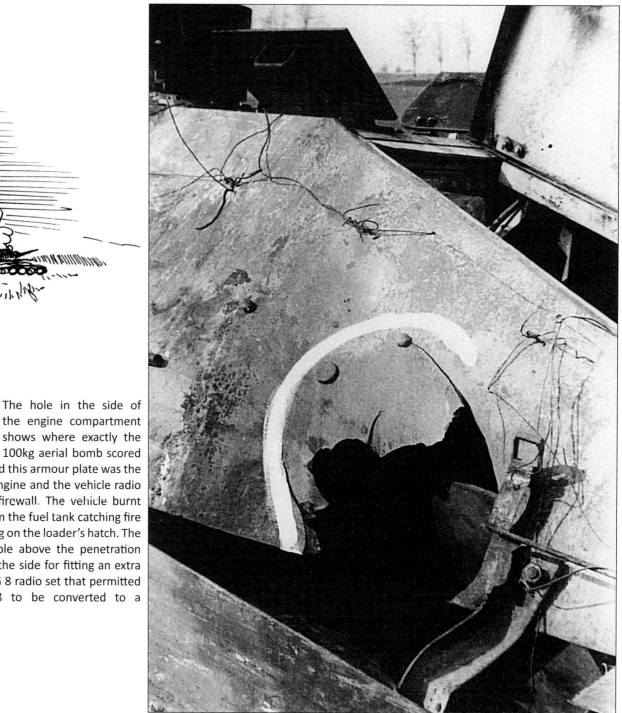

250 At the edge of the forest northwest of Füle, a late production Hummel destroyed by an ROFS-132 rocket that, according to the Russian technical report, had detonated the stowed ammunition. The barrel, broken at the breech, looks very much like the work of a demolition charge. This Hummel was lost on 22 March 1945, but because all five Panzer-Divisions trapped in the pocket northeast of Balaton (5.SS, 9.SS, 1., 3. and 23.) possessed these vehicles, it is difficult to pin down the unit with any certainty. However, vehicles from SS-Pz.Art.Rgt.9 (9.SS) were known to have carried two spare roadwheels on the rear of the fighting compartment as this vehicle has. The rear hull plate shows part of a hard edged camouflage pattern.

251 Jenő, about 6km north of the Hummel on the previous page, where this Wespe was destroyed on 22 March 1945 by direct hit from a FAB-100. Not only has the back-end been obliterated, but the side wall has buckled, bending what should be a straight run of track. The Russians have chalked *"Ucht. 3"* (Count.[ed] 3) on a hull side plate that has swung out with the force of the blast. In the background is a Hummel with trophy number '252' seen on the next page.

252 The Hummel from the background of page 63, also destroyed by direct hit from a FAB-100 which apparently set the fuel tank on fire. Both tracks have snaked forward, possibly indicating that the vehicle was moving forward when hit, the drive sprockets continuing to turn for a second or two. It is a late production vehicle with full width driver's and radio operator's compartment which has a scruffy coat of whitewash.

253 The southern edge of Jenő, and another late production Hummel destroyed by direct hit from a FAB-100 in the fighting compartment. The bomb had detonated under the vehicle, with inevitably catastrophic results. Like the vehicle on page 62, this appears to have a hard edged camouflage pattern on the side wall and an extra camouflage loop, next to the trophy umber '253'. The object sticking out the back of the weapon like a scorpion tail is the gun's recoil slide.

 254 Northwest of Füle, a self-propelled howitzer battery was attacked from the air while in a firing position. This Wespe probably belonged to 4./SS-Pz.Art.Rgt.5 of 5.SS-Panzer-Division and like the previous SP artillery was knocked out on 22 March 1945. It was destroyed by a 37mm aircraft-cannon round that penetrated the engine compartment, note the large hole on the glacis plate next to the driver's compartment. The vehicle still has the remains of a whitewash over its paintwork and carries two spare roadwheels. The Wespe in the background, trophy number '255', does not appear in the Russian report and so is not included in this book.

258 Wespe undressed. PTAB bombs and RS rockets have blown this Wespe's fighting compartment apart. The location is Sándorka, roughly 2·5km northwest of Füle, so it is possible that this Wespe belonged to the same unit and was destroyed on the same date as the vehicle on the previous page. The top of the driver's compartment has been destroyed and the muzzle brake deformed. The picture offers a unique view of the inside of the left wall.

261 Another dead Wespe destroyed by Sturmoviks near Sándorka on 22 March 1945. The style and location of the tactical number are the same as the Wespe on page 66, so we assume that it also belonged to 5./SS-Pz.Art. Rgt.5 of 5.SS-Panzer-Division. The lower corner of the left armoured wall was penetrated by 23mm round from a VYa air cannon. Several craters from PTAB bombs were visible within a metre of the vehicle.

264 This Hummel, with separate compartment for the driver and old cast hub caps, is shown west of Erzsébetpuszta (south of Jenő) after being destroyed by an ROFS-132 rocket in the forward part of the engine compartment. We think that by engine compartment they mean the rear of the vehicle which was the fighting compartment (the engine was mounted in the middle, under the gun). Another ROFS-132 exploded immediately behind the vehicle. Like other AFVs shown in this book, it was knocked out on 22 March 1945 - a bad day for the Panzerwaffe in Hungary. Without other views we cannot say for certain if this was a Hummel or Munitionspanzer Hummel, since there is no gun. The Russians have not finished the trophy number on the side. Or perhaps it means something else?

269 A Panzer IV/70(V) belly-deep in a farmer's field near the forest west of Sándorka. Fragments of an ROFS-132 rocket penetrated the engine compartment and set the fuel tanks on fire, which in turn 'cooked off' the ammunition, blowing the roof off the fighting compartment which has jammed itself into the ground. The Russians have marked a white circle on the side of the engine deck which is probably where the rocket struck. The vehicle was knocked out on 22 March 1945, but the unit is unknown.

 'Totalausfall' (total loss). Northwest of Sándorka, a le.S.P.W. Sd.Kfz.250 Ausf.B strafed by 20mm aircraft cannon and reduced to a kit of parts by a direct hit from an ROFS-132 rocket. The rear compartment has been completely destroyed and the armour next to the co-driver swung out at an angle. Radios and their racks can be seen in the foreground along with a muzzle brake from a 7,5cm Pak 40. No trophy number is noted in the report or visible on the wreck.

281 North of Füle, a Jagdpanzer IV has been destroyed by a direct hit from a FAB-100 bomb on the roof of the fighting compartment, the resulting explosion has unseated the superstructure and probably set off the stowed ammunition. The Jagdpanzer looks to be assembled around July 1944 as it has a modified (lightened) gun mount, larger conical MG cover and 'Zimmerit' coating. The location and 'Zimmerit' suggest that the vehicle belonged to Pz.Jg.Abt.543 of 3.Panzer-Division (who were issued 21 vehicles in early August 1944.) The vehicle was knocked out on 22-23 March 1945.

283 The turret roof, complete with commander's cupola attached has been blown off this Pz.Kpfw.IV Ausf.J north of Füle, the work of 37mm aircraft cannon penetrating the turret roof. Fire has then consumed the wreck, as all of the tyres have been reduced to ash and there is significant charring. It is possible that this Panzer is from the same unit as the Pz.Kpfw.IV on page 28, because the method of applying spare tracks to the drive's front plate is the same.

286 On the Nádasdladány - Sárszentmihály road, a Pz.Beob.Wg.III blown apart by PTAB bombs on 21-22 March 1945, its superstructure straddling the roadside ditch. The tactical number on the turret 'Schürze' reads '501' or '601', which suggests it was from II./Pz.Art.Rgt.75 of 3.Panzer-Division, although 1. and 23.Panzer-Division were also equipped with these observation vehicles. The Russian report states that the tank had been blown apart by stowed ammunition exploding, but the gun was a dummy and the only ammunition was for the ball-mounted MG 34 in the turret and two MP38s, unless one of the demolition charges blew up?

296 Southeast of Zámoly, the side armour of this Panther was penetrated by a 37mm aircraft-cannon round causing the ammunition to explode and blowing the turret off. The Panther, which is an M.A.N. Ausf.G from June or July 1944, probably belonged to I./Pz.Rgt.1 of 1.Panzer-Division, although 3. and 23.Panzer-Division were also in the area. We presume it was on 11 January 1945, when Soviet Sturmoviks inflicted heavy losses on the attacking German Panzers. The whitewash is clearly visible on the hull and gun barrel.

A Tiger I, two Wespe and a Panther, all from 3.SS-Panzer-Division, at a Russian collection point in Baracksa. The Tiger is the same vehicle as shown on pages 34 and 35 of Panzerwrecks 7 and was lost 1·5km southwest of Pettend after an 85mm tank round penetrated its frontal armour. It was assigned the trophy number '60' by the 'artillery' commission of the 3rd Ukrainian Front. The Panther was an early Ausf.G with 'Zimmerit'. It had trophy number '87' (also assigned by the 'artillery' commission of the 3rd Ukrainian Front) and was also destroyed by an 85mm tank round, which penetrated the left side of the turret. The Panther burned out and two charred bodies were subsequently found inside. All of the vehicles in this photo were destroyed between 22 and 30 January 1945.

298 Southeast of Zámoly, a Tiger II of s.H.Pz.Abt.'Feldherrnhalle' destroyed by an ROFS-132 rocket that hit the corner of the turret. Furthermore, the gun barrel was struck by a 45mm anti-tank round and the idler wheel on the opposite side destroyed. The crew have drained the recoil system of fluids and the gun fired one last time, rendering it useless and making it look shorter. The Tiger was lost on 11 January 1945 and not far from it was another, a victim of Soviet artillery. It had trophy number '300' and appears on page 65 of Panzerwrecks 7.

Hein

298

RODNA

309A

This Bergepanther was knocked out southeast of Zámoly, by 37mm aircraft-cannon fire through the side armour. We presume that it was destroyed on 11 January 1945, along with the Panzers from the previous pages. The Bergepanther was assembled by Seibert-Stahlbau of Aschaffenberg, and has all the hallmarks of a vehicle converted from a Panther returned for rebuilding in 1945. Seibert Bergepanthers were referred to as 'Umbau Bergepanther' and were much simpler and quicker to produce than their Henschel, Daimler-Benz and Demag counterparts, lacking the winch, spade and pusher bars.

315A A Sturmgeschütz III Ausf.G of 3.SS-Panzer-Division destroyed by PTAB bombs southeast of Mór between 16 and 18 March 1945. The bombs penetrated the roof armour and detonated the stowed ammunition. The tracks stowed on the side of the superstructure are 'Winterketten' and being wider, gave better flotation on soft ground. The charring inside the opened engine hatches would indicate that the engine caught fire.

316A

A 40.M Nimród of the Hungarian 2.Armoured Division between Mór and Söréd and probably lost between 16 and 18 March 1945. Although not immediately obvious due to the quality of the photo, the side of the superstructure is missing.

317A Another 3.SS-Panzer-Division Sturmgeschütz III, this one 100 metres southwest of Söréd, destroyed by PTAB bombs to the hull and the engine compartment. It had been stuck in the mud when spotted by Sturmoviks and attacked; around the assault gun were up to fifteen craters made by PTAB and AO-25 bombs. In the background are two more wrecked Sturmgeschütze that do not appear in the report. It is likely that they were part of a counterattack that was halted between 16 and 18 March 1945.

327A 24 March 1945, Márkó, a village northwest of Veszprém. A headless Panther from I./SS-Pz.Rgt.1 or I./SS Pz. Rgt.12 that looks like it has been destroyed by its crew. A fire in the engine compartment has blackened much of the rear wall, but not consumed the tyres on the roadwheels. Crews were trained to place demolition charges in the engine and fighting compartments, and the damage (flipped turret, wrecked driver's compartment and engine fire) is consistent with this. M.A.N. completed the Panther on November/December 1944 and is one of the few completed by them after October to be fitted with the original 600mm idler.

Looking like a partially built model kit is this Sd.Kfz.7/2 which was destroyed by an ROFS-132 south of Jenő. An explosion, whether from the rocket or vehicle's ammunition, has all but stripped the gun and blown the armoured cab apart, leaving only the fire wall and a couple of doors. A 300mm riser has been fitted to the platform to enable the gun to fire over the armoured cab.

338A

A rare-breed Sd.Kfz.7/2 (armed with a 3,7cm Flak 43, rather than the more commonly seen Flak 36) destroyed by machinegun and cannon fire from Sturmoviks on the Veszprém - Városlőd road, near Herend on 23 or 24 March 1945. The Russian technical team noted that the vehicle had been hit four times by 37mm cannon fire and burnt out. The Sd.Anh.57 (1 Achs) für Zubehör und Munition für 3,7cm Flak (Sfl) trailer (still hitched) carried accessories and ammunition. Ammunition boxes and spent cases litter the scene and pay testament to a fierce, but ultimately futile, defence.

338A What we think is the 3,7cm Flak 43 equipped Sd.Kfz.7/2 from the previous page, although the original Russian report gives a different location of 1km north of Balatonfőkajár, not Herend. The number '7' has been painted behind the driver's door and the tactical insignia for a Flak (Sfl.) unit is visible on the rear. A dead crewman lies to the left of the picture.

344A

There's not much left of this Panzer IV/70(V). Superstructure, engine, wheels, tracks - all gone. The vehicle, we think, belonged to SS-Pz.Jg.Abt.1, 1.SS-Panzer-Division and was destroyed on 25-26 March 1945 in Bakonygyepes by two PTAB bombs in the engine compartment. The vehicle subsequently caught fire and set off the ammunition. The dishevelled look of the building (a pub) in the background is consistent with there being an exploding armoured vehicle on the doorstep.

353A

A Marder38T found at Apácatorna, about 10km east of Jánosházas, destroyed by 23mm cannon fire from Sturmoviks on 26-27 March 1945. The top of the hull and front of the fighting compartment have been blown out, leaving charring around the air intake on the side and blistering the paint of the one remaining wall of the fighting compartment. Note the anti-tank mine sitting under the front of the vehicle. Pz.Jg.Abt.37 of 1.Panzer-Division was the most likely user.

402 1km east of Devecser, a late production Sturmgeschütz III Ausf.G with co-axial MG destroyed by PTAB bombs. Although from this angle the vehicle looks fairly intact, in reality it was severely damaged: the PTAB bombs had shattered the chassis and penetrated the commander's hatch; the crew compartment had burned out completely (note the charring around the back end). The faint remains of a tactical number can be seen on the side but are too indistinct to make out. Nevertheless, given the location, it can safely be concluded that the assault gun belonged to 1.SS-Panzer-Division and was lost on 25-26 March 1945.

The smashed remains of a m.S.P.W. (Sd.Kfz.251) destroyed by an AO-25 fragmentation bomb in a farmer's field northeast of Székesfehérvár. Areas of the nose armour have been holed and the rear section has separated from the front, revealing a fire damaged interior. Part of the tactical number '84' is visible on the side. It is likely that it was lost on 23-24 December and belonged to 3.Panzer-Division.

A m.S.P.W. (Sd.Kfz.251) lies burnt out in a cornfield south of Jenő after being hit by an ROFS-132 rocket on 21-22 March 1945. Fire has burnt the paintwork at the top of the hull sides and MG shield, but despite this its tactical number '2101' remains visible, painted in a white outline. It is a late production vehicle with separate engine and radiator access hatches.

RODNA

Like the other prime movers shown in this book, this Sd.Kfz.7, with a plank of wood under or replacing the engine, has had its front wheels removed. It was destroyed in the area of Berhida by an RS-82 rocket on 21-22 March 1945.

t looks very much like the engine of this Sd.Kfz.8, from an unknown Luftwaffe unit, exploded after being strafed by Sturmoviks on the road from Balatonfőkajár to Füle. Note the pennant painted onto the front fender and horseshoe above it.

Soviet soldiers inspect the wrecks at Balatonfűzfő railway station shortly after the area was overrun by the Red Army. By then it had taken on the appearance of a scrap yard, because the Germans had collected a large number of wrecks in attempt to evacuate as many damaged AFVs by rail as possible. The Soviets collected still more.

The vehicle in the foreground is a Marder 38T from Pz.Jg.Abt.37, 1.Panzer-Division and is notable for having a mount for a machinegun welded to the top of the gun mount. Immediately behind is a Sturmgeschütz.III Ausf.G, tactical number '3202', which arrived in Hungary in January 1945 as part of Heeres-Sturmartillerie-Brigade.303. The Panther on the left is '212' (trophy number '35') shown on page 21. Viewed from this angle, we can see that the gun mantlet has been penetrated by an AP round in addition to the hole in the hull, just below the trophy number and has lost its tracks and a number of roadwheels. Behind the Panther is a Pz.Kpfw.IV with the number '22' on the turret side and a Jagdpanther. The hull to the right of the Marder is a Universal Carrier, probably used by the Soviets. Further back are a pair of Flakpanzer IV 'Wirbelwinds', Panthers, Sturmgeschütz and T-34s.